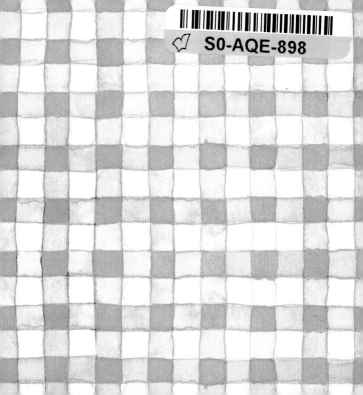

A Special Gift

for: _____

_____

from: _____

_____

date: _____

Copyright © 2001
The Brownlow Corporation
6309 Airport Freeway
Fort Worth, Texas 76117

Illustration © 2001 Audrey Jeanne Roberts

Written and Illustrated by
Audrey Jeanne Roberts

Edited by Rhonda S. Hogan

Designed by Melissa Reagan

ISBN 1-57051-967-6

Printed in China

The Gift of Friendship

A Joy Shared

Written and Illustrated by Audrey Jeanne Roberts

Brownlow

Little Treasures
Miniature Books

One of the most delightful aspects of friendship is that there is no way to have one unless you share it with someone else!

A friend loves at all times.

PROVERBS 17:17

Even the simple, ordinary things in our daily lives become more special when we share them with our friends ~ Coffee, tea, or a quiet time in the garden with a gently blowing breeze.

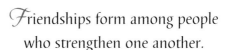

Friendships form among people who strengthen one another.

FRANKLIN OWEN

We cannot tell the precise
moment when friendship is formed.
As in filling a vessel drop by drop,
there is at least a drop which makes
it run over; so in a series of kindnesses
there is at least one which
makes the heart run over.

SAMUEL JOHNSON

My life is a chronicle of friendship. My friends—all those about me—create my world anew each day. Without their loving care, all the courage I could summon would not suffice to keep my heart strong for life. But, like Stevenson, I know it is better to do things than to imagine them.

HELEN KELLER

A friend shares her counsel and encouragement. She helps you see life from a different vantage point. Sometimes she can even help you see the humorous side of a difficult situation!

Be devoted to one another in brotherly love. Honor one another above yourselves.

ROMANS 12:10

Joy grows when life is shared with Family & Friends

Joy of the Lord is my strength

Sharing burdens with a friend doesn't weigh her down ~ a shared load is a lighter load. Sharing your burdens gives you the strength to carry on and the endurance to finish the race. Then when her turn comes, you'll be ready to return the favor!

When friends walk beside us
On the trails that we must keep,

Our burdens seem less heavy
And the hills are not so steep.

The weary miles pass swiftly
Taken in a joyous stride,

And all the world seems brighter
When friends walk by our side.

ANONYMOUS

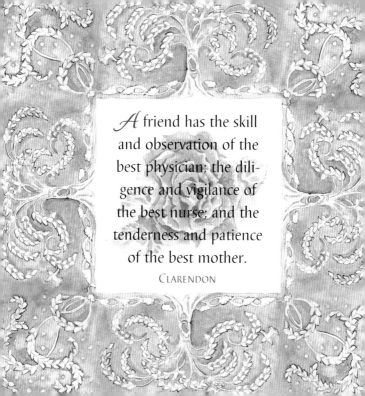

A friend has the skill
and observation of the
best physician; the dili-
gence and vigilance of
the best nurse; and the
tenderness and patience
of the best mother.

CLARENDON

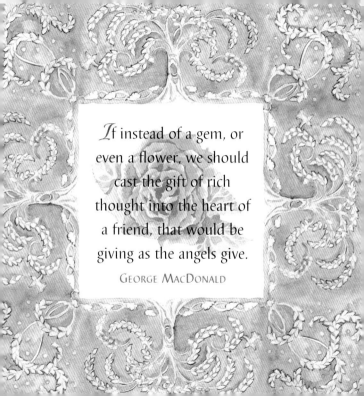

If instead of a gem, or
even a flower, we should
cast the gift of rich
thought into the heart of
a friend, that would be
giving as the angels give.

GEORGE MACDONALD

One of the things I love to do most with my special friend is share the memories of the times we've spent together. It always amazes me that she remembers different things than I do. Together we have double the memories to treasure!

The comfort of having
a friend may be taken
away, but not that
of having had one.

SENECA

Traveling in the company
of those we love is
home in motion.

LEIGH HUNT

Sharing laughter, being silly, enjoying an inside joke ~ these are some of the best parts of friendship. Laughter refreshes. Laughter renews. Laughter is a gift from God that brings healing to the hurting heart.

No life is so strong and complete, but it yearns for the smile of a friend.

WALLACE BRUCE

Shopping, folding laundry, cooking dinner, weeding a garden. Even the everyday, ordinary tasks of life are more fun when shared together.

*F*riendship improves happiness,
and abates misery, by doubling
our joy, and dividing our grief.

JOSEPH ADDISON

*T*wo are better than one, because
they have a good return for their work.

ECCLESIASTES 4:9

Lifelong friends are special.
Growing up together and then
growing old together is so much fun.
It's nice to keep people in our lives
that remember what we looked like
when we were skinny, had no wrinkles,
or gray hair!

To have a friend is to have one of the sweetest gifts that life can bring; to be a friend is to have a solemn and tender education of soul from day to day.

AMY ROBERTSON BROWN

Old friends, old scenes will lovelier be
As more of heaven in each we see.

JOHN KEBLE

Sometimes even best friends
have no words. There is a
special joy in simply
being comfortable in
each other's
presence.

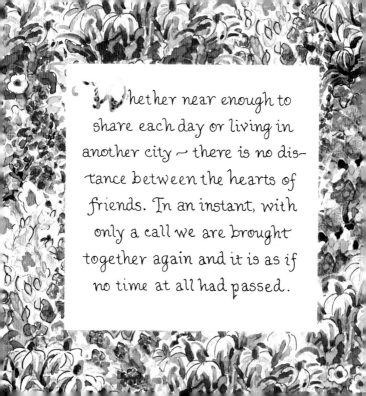

Whether near enough to share each day or living in another city ~ there is no distance between the hearts of friends. In an instant, with only a call we are brought together again and it is as if no time at all had passed.

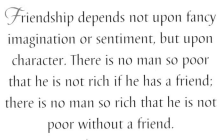

Friendship depends not upon fancy
imagination or sentiment, but upon
character. There is no man so poor
that he is not rich if he has a friend;
there is no man so rich that he is not
poor without a friend.

ANONYMOUS

A true friend sticks closer than
one's nearest kin.

PROVERBS 18:24 (NRSV)

*T*rue friendship comes when silence
between two people is comfortable.

DAVE TYSON GENTRY

*T*he language of friendship is not words,
but meanings. It is an intelligence
above language.

HENRY DAVID THOREAU

*E*veryone hears what you say.
Friends listen to what you say.
Best friends listen to what you don't say.

There is no joy like a joy that is shared. Friends delight in each other's successes. They savor the other's accomplishments as much as their own. They love to brag about each other!

Friends are a very rare jewel. They make you smile and encourage you to succeed. They lend an ear, they share a word of praise, and they always want to open their hearts to you.

Dreaming about the future together is one of my favorite things to share. My best friend and I have had the joy of seeing many of those dreams come to be. That gives us the faith to keep believing and dreaming. Together we reach towards tomorrow and all the blessings it holds.

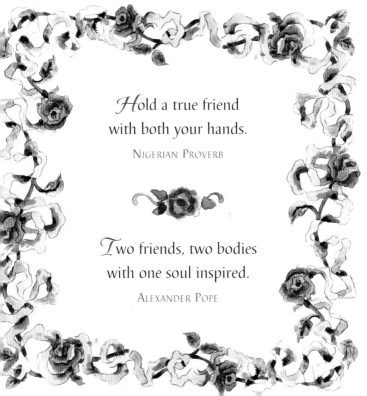

*H*old a true friend
with both your hands.

NIGERIAN PROVERB

*T*wo friends, two bodies
with one soul inspired.

ALEXANDER POPE

A friend that is trustworthy ~ who keeps your confidences ~ is a gift from God. She listens. She cares.

She lifts your burdens before him in prayer.

It is my joy in life to find
    At every turning of the road,

The strong arms of a comrade kind
    To help me onward with my load;

And since I have no gold to give,
    And love alone must make amends,

My only prayer is, while I live—
    God make me worthy
        of my friends.

FRANK D. SHERMAN

A friend helps you see yourself as others do. She's like a mirror that reflects back to you the essence of who you are, but she does it gently!

Every good and perfect gift is from above.

JAMES 1:17

A friend senses a need often even before she's called. She's there in a crisis, providing a shoulder to cry on, and an arm to lean on.

*O*ther blessings may be taken away,
but if we have acquired a good friend
by goodness, we have a blessing which
improves in value when others fail. It
is even heightened by sufferings.

W.E. CHANNING

*S*hare with God's people who are
in need. Practice hospitality.

ROMANS 12:13

A friend cares more about you than your house! She looks past the weeds in your garden and marvels at the roses. In turn, she's comfortable enough to let you have tea in her kitchen even if there are dishes in her sink.

A friend loves you enough to tell you the truth, but is merciful enough to NOT tell you all of it! She treasures your best qualities while overlooking your flaws!

You can always tell a real friend: when you've made a fool of yourself, he doesn't feel you've done a permanent job.

LAURENCE J. PETER

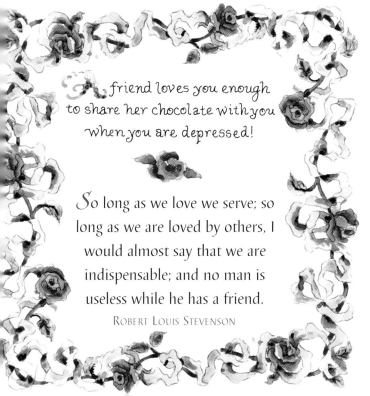

A friend loves you enough to share her chocolate with you when you are depressed!

So long as we love we serve; so long as we are loved by others, I would almost say that we are indispensable; and no man is useless while he has a friend.

ROBERT LOUIS STEVENSON

A joy shared, the gift
of friendship treasured.
Its value grows greater
with every year that passes.
I'm so glad that you have
shared your life with me.
Thank you for being such
a wonderful friend!